Table of Contents

Introductioin 3

What is an herb? 4

    Fresh herbs and plants you can grow that are great to have handy in the kitchen. 4

Fresh vs. Dried 5

    Kitchen herb garden Growing your own 6

    What to look for when buying 7

    How to cut herbs 7

    How to store fresh herbs 8

    How to wash fresh herbs 8

    How to chop fresh herbs 9

    When to add fresh herbs 9

Recipes 20

    Spiced Grilled Chicken with Cilantro Butter 20

    Rosemary Salmon and Veggies 21

    Orange Blossom Mint Refresher 23

    Blueberry, Basil and Goat Cheese Pie 24

    Herbed Feta Dip 26

    Cauliflower Dill Kugel 27

    Cinnamon-Basil Ice Cream 29

    Flaky Biscuits with Herb Butter 31

Chicken and Broccoli with Dill Sauce 33

Cheddar and Chive Mashed Potatoes 35

Golden Beet and Peach Soup with Tarragon 37

Rosemary and Ginger Infused Water 39

Herbed Tuna and White Bean Salad 39

Cilantro Lime Shrimp 41

Basil Salt 43

Dilly Cheese Ball 43

Green Beans and Radish Salad with Tarragon Pesto 44

Peach-Basil Lemonade Slush 46

Apricot-Rosemary Scones 47

Honey-Thyme Butter 49

Bottom line 50

Introductioin

Cooking with fresh herbs isn't just for gourmet chefs.Learn everything you need to know about buying, preparing, storing and cooking with herbs. A lot of people are intimidated by the idea of using fresh herbs in their cooking. You've heard that fresh is best, but if you don't have a lot of experience with herbs then you'll probably have a few questions. Which herbs pair with which types of food? How much should I use? When do I add them to the cooking process? What should I do with the leftovers?

Although there are a few occasions when using dried herbs is recommended,cooking with fresh seems to be the preference for many chefs. They're flavorful, make beautiful garnishes and most importantly, they're packed with valuable nutrients and antioxidants. With a few tips and tricks you can maximize your use of fresh herbs to transform every meal into something special.

When summer arrives, its time to fire up the grill and load up on picnic-basket favorites.But a good cook will tell you it's also the best time to shelve that old jar of dried seasoning. Why? Fresh herbs such as basil, cilantro and thyme are at their peak freshness.Herbs are an easy way to add life to dull dishes.As such, they're the secret weapon for many professional cooks. These tasty little plants add vitality to every bite. Toss some basil into a caprese salad or garnish tacos with fresh cilantro and your family might just start calling you chef.

What is an herb?

Herbs are the leafy parts of plants that do not have woody stems. They can be fresh or dried. Dried herbs have a stronger flavour than fresh but lose their strength quickly.

Fresh herbs and plants you can grow that are great to have handy in the kitchen.

Parsley

Parsley is a mild bitter herb that can enhance the flavor of your foods. Many consider parsley just to be a curly green garnish for food, but it actually helps things like stews achieve a more balanced flavor. As an added benefit, parsley can aid in digestion. Parsley is often grown as an annual, but in milder climates, it will stay evergreen all winter long. Parsley plants will grow to be large and bushy. Parsley is a good source of Vitamins A and C.

Mint

There are several varieties of mint. You can use it in drinks like mojitos or mint juleps. Or add some mint to your summer iced tea. Mint freshens the breath and will help to calm your stomach. But if you grow mint, remember that it's considered an invasive plant. Mint will spread and take over your garden. It's best grown in containers.

Dill

Dill is a great flavoring for fish, lamb, potatoes, and peas. It also aids in digestion, helps to fight bad breath and has the added benefits of reducing swelling and cramps. Dill is easy to grow. It will also attract helpful insects to your garden such as wasps and other predatory insects. It also saves a trip to the Dentist Santa Barbara!

Fresh vs. Dried

Choosing between fresh or dried herbs is a matter of preference. Some chefs advise against using fresh when cooking a dish that needs to simmer longer than 45 minutes. Dried herbs pack a stronger, more condensed flavor, so if you're substituting dried herbs in the place of fresh, then you'll need to cut the amount in half.

Dried herbs do have a few pitfalls, however. They will eventually lose their flavor over time and should be replaced at least once a year. There is also evidence that suggests a substantial amount of nutrients are lost in the drying process.

Although fresh herbs tend to have a softer flavor, subtlety when cooking is not necessarily a bad thing. Most chefs strive for a well balanced blend of flavors so that a particular ingredient does not dominate the dish.

Kitchen herb garden Growing your own

Growing your own herbs gives you certain advantages over buying them from the market. Cutting sprigs moments before use ensures maximum flavor and nutrition, and you waste less since you're only cutting what you need.

Every herb plant is unique and requires slightly different harvesting techniques. It's always a good idea to snip the leaves using scissors rather than pulling them off with your fingers. Start by removing older leaves from the outside of the plant to encourage growth. Then work your way inward toward the younger stems.

What to look for when buying

If you have to purchase your herbs from a grocery store, try to pick them up as close to your cooking time as possible. Look for bunches with vibrant color and aroma. Herbs packed in plastic should be pried open for a sniff test. If you can't smell them then chances are you won't be able to taste them.

Avoid limp and soggy bundles with any discoloration in the form of black spots or general yellowing. Grocery stores often overspray their produce to give the illusion of freshness, when in fact, excessive watering encourages rot and mold.

How to cut herbs

If you're not using yours herbs immediately then you'll want to pretreat them before you place them back in the refrigerator. First remove anything fastening your herbs together. Ties and rubber bands can bruise fragile plants affecting their longevity and flavor.

The root ends will need to be snipped as they will draw moisture away from the leaves resulting in premature wilting. If the roots are substantial then you can save them for soup or curry flavoring.

How to store fresh herbs

Before you store your herbs in the fridge, wrap them in a slightly damp paper towel and put them in a ziplock bag. Make sure the bag has a little bit of air inside, and place it in the warmest part of your fridge (usually located either in the doors or on the top shelf). When you're ready to use your herbs, just cut away any wilted or discolored leaves. Fresh herbs don't have a long shelf life so use them as soon as possible.

How to wash fresh herbs

Not having to wash your herbs is another benefit of growing your own. Water will quicken their demise, so if you can, skip this step. Only wash your herbs if you're going to use them immediately, otherwise store them in your fridge unwashed.

Fill a bowl with cold water and place your herbs inside. Gently move them around the water to remove any dirt. If there is a significant amount of sediment at the bottom of the bowl, dump your water and give the herbs another rinse. Gently pat them dry using a paper towel or give them a whirl in a salad spinner.

How to chop fresh herbs

A really sharp knife is a worthwhile investment and makes preparing food a more enjoyable experience. Whether you're throwing your herbs into a food processor or you're chopping them by hand, ensure that the blade you are using is sharpened. A dull blade will bruise your herbs, changing the color of your leaves from a vibrant green to a dull black. Scissors can also be used if you're not concerned about achieving small, uniform pieces.

To maximize the flavor of your herbs you'll want to chop them as finely as possible. The finer you chop your herbs, the more oils released and the more fragrant the herb will become. Delicate herbs like parsley and cilantro should be chopped right before use as they will lose their aroma quickly. It's often recommended to add these more delicate herbs after you've taken your dish off the heat or right before serving.

When to add fresh herbs

When to add fresh herbs to your cooking depends not only on the herb but also on the sort of flavor you're trying to achieve. Robust herbs like rosemary, thyme and savory can be used in longer simmering dishes. Gently bruise the leaves with your fingers before dropping them in to release more oils and increase flavor.

Adding herbs at the beginning of your cooking will create a subtle background note. If at the end you find you want to punch up the flavor, just add a bit more for reinforcement. Remember, you don't want any one flavor to stand out too much.

If you keep the leaves on their stem they will be easier to remove later. Using an herb sachet, also known as a bouquet garni, is another option that will keep you from losing your herbs in a sauce or broth. This also allows you to control the flavor if you find the herbs are becoming overpowering.

Leftovers

Because fresh herbs don't have a long shelf life after they've been cut, it's a good idea to use them all as soon as possible. Knowing what types of herbs pair with which types of foods will allow you to be flexible and creative in the kitchen. You could also infuse oils with your leftover herbs or add them to cocktails. The possibilities are endless!

Basil

Whether you choose large leaf Italian basis or large purple sweet basil, this plant is popular in many cuisines but is a feature in Italian cooking like pizzas, salads, sauces, and pesto. Some people think basil is great for planting alongside your tomatoes but there's no real evidence that it makes your tomatoes taste sweeter. Basil has health benefits of antioxidants and is a defense against low blood sugar.

Sage

Sage is an aromatic herb that is great for seasoning meats, sauces, and vegetables. But be careful because sage will have a tendency to overpower other flavors. Sage also helps to relieve cuts, inflammation and helps with memory issues. It was once thought to be a medicinal cure-all. Sage is an easy herb to grow and is relatively easy to care for. It's great in your garden for attracting bees.

Rosemary

Rosemary is one of the most flavorful herbs and is great for adding to things like poultry, meats, and vegetables. Around Christmastime, you'll see tree-shaped rosemary bushes for sale. You can bring them home and keep them for planting in the spring. The fragrant plant is a delightful scent and is sometimes used in floral arrangements. Rosemary likes its soil a bit on the dry side, so be careful not to overwater. Allowed to flourish, a rosemary plant will grow into a full-sized bush. For more guidedance, be sure to check out this guide titled, 'How I grew a rosemary plant in my garden'!

Thyme

Thyme is a delicate looking plant. It is often used for flavoring egg, bean and vegetable dishes. Thyme is frequently used in the Mediterranean, Italian and Provençal French cuisines. Pair it with lamb, poultry, and tomatoes. Thyme is often added to soups and stews. Thyme is part of the mint family. The most common variety is garden thyme which has gray-green leaves and a minty, somewhat lemony smell.

Cilantro/Coriander

Cilantro is also known as coriander leaf or Chinese parsley. Cilantro is perfect for adding into spicy foods like chills, and Mexican, Chinese, Southeast Asian and Indian cuisines. The seeds of cilantro are known as coriander. The plant grows early in the season and doesn't like it when the ground becomes too warm.

Fennel

Fennel is very flavorful and aromatic, and along with anise is a primary ingredient in absinthe. Fennel is native to the Mediterranean region and does best in dry soils near the ocean or on river banks. The strongly flavored leaves of fennel are similar in shape to dill. The bulb can be sautéed or grilled, or eaten raw. Fennel bulbs are used for garnishes or sometimes added to salads.

Chamomile

In the United States and Europe, chamomile is most often used as an ingredient in herbal tea. It is one of the world's most widely consumed herbal teas. But it has also been used for thousands of years as a traditional medicine for settling stomachs and calming the nerves. Chamomile also helps reduce inflammation and treat fevers. You can grow either German chamomile or Roman chamomile. The two are interchangeable when it comes to making tea, but they are grown very differently. German chamomile is an annual plant that grows up to three feet tall. Roman chamomile is a perennial but only grows to about a foot high. German chamomile is more commonly known for its blossoms.

French Tarragon

Fresh tarragon is the traditional ingredient of 'Fines Herbes' and is the aristocrat of fresh herbs. A must-have for any Culinary Herb Garden! It will transform an ordinary dish into a work of art with it's spicy anise flavor. A little tarragon in a chicken salad makes a profound difference. It is wonderful in sauces, soups and meat dishes. Try it with vegetables. It is the choice for any hearty dish.

Lavender

Grown as a condiment and for use in salads and dressings, lavender will give most dishes a slightly sweet flavor. Lavender syrup and dried lavender buds are used in the United States for making lavender scones and marshmallows. Health benefits include the soothing of insect bites and headaches when used with herbs and aromatherapy. Lavender plants will survive in many growing conditions but do best in full sun in warm, well-drained soil.

Catnip

What's more fun than seeing the family cat go slightly berserk over the smell of catnip? But catnip is more than a feline stimulant. It can be used as a relaxing agent as well as a diuretic and laxative. If you plant catnip outside, remember that cats do love to roll in it and chew on it. But keeping catnip in your garden can also be a deterrent for rodents. If the cat's around, the pests most likely won't be.

Chives are a member of the garlic family and can be the perfect complement to sour cream. Chives are mostly used for flavoring and are considered one of the "fine herbs" of French cuisine. Chives are native to Asia but have been used as an additive to food for almost 5,000 years. Chives work well with eggs, fish, potatoes, salads, shellfish, and soups. Chives are an excellent source of beta carotene and Vitamin C.

St. John's Wort

St. John's wort is believed to alleviate the symptoms of depression and anxiety, but should not be considered a cure. It can also help fight muscle pain. The word "wort" is an Old English word for "plant." The plant was named because the flowers appear around June 24th which is the birthday of John the Baptist. St. John's wort is also known as Tipton's weed, rosin rose, goatweed, chase-devil or Klamath weed. In gardens, it's a popular groundcover since it is drought tolerant. While not used in cooking it is a well-known herbal treatment for depression.

Bay Leaves

The smell of bay's noble leaves reminds you of balsam, clove, mint, and some say even honey! Well known for its use in hearty stews and other long-simmering dishes with a slightly sharp, peppery, almost bitter taste. Add the whole leaves at the beginning of the cooking process and remember to remove them before serving. Sweet bay is native to the Mediterranean.

Nope, I didn't say cilantro, this is its cousin culantro. You can use this wherever 'Cilantro' is called for, with its spicy and pungent flavor, a wonderful addition to any dish, fresh or dried. Some call it 'Mexican Corriander' or 'Chadon beni'. Culantro is a rare and unusual herb in the USA, but it's well known in Vietnam, Latin American and all over the Caribbean.

Chervil

Chervil produces flat, light-green, lacy leaves with a hint of anise, and enhances the flavor of chicken, fish, vegetables, eggs, and salads. It is an heirloom herb that was most likely introduced to European herb gardening by the Romans. Closely related to Parsley, chervil has become an indispensable herb plant in the kitchen, and a classic among herb plants in French cuisine.

Winter Savory

A deliciously spicy culinary herb, Winter Savory adds an aromatic flavor to many dishes. Also used medicinally for its antibacterial and anti-fungal properties. Winter Savory, like its Summer counterpart, is a spicy culinary herb from the Mint family that compliments fish, beans, and poultry with its intense flavor. Though it loses some of this intensity during the cooking process, Winter Savory remains aromatic and is often used to flavor liqueurs and makes a beautiful garnish to any salad.

Peppermint

Like other mints, peppermint is known for aiding digestion and freshening the breath. But peppermint is also a good source of calcium, potassium and Vitamin B. Peppermint is a hybrid mint, being a cross between water mint and spearmint. Peppermint oil can be used for flavoring but is also useful as a natural pesticide. It has been shown to reduce the effects of irritable bowel syndrome. Peppermint prefers rich soil and partial shade. Like other mints, it spreads quickly, so consider planting it in containers.

Stevia

Stevia is an attractive looking plant and a natural sweetener. The added benefit is that there are no calories. Stevia is part of the sunflower family and is native to subtropical and tropical regions in the Western hemisphere. While it's a perennial plant it will only survive in the milder climates in North America. Still, you can add stevia to your garden for the summer. It is also known as sweetleaf or sugarleaf and is grown for its sweet leaves. Stevia can be used as a natural sweetener and as a sugar substitute.

Aloe Vera is known for its soothing properties for burns or skin problems. Many people keep an Aloe Vera plant handy in the kitchen for incidental burns. But taken orally, Aloe Vera will also help with digestion, circulation and weight loss. There are over 250 species of Aloes. Most of these are native to Africa. Aloe Vera plants are very succulent and are as much as 95% water. That means they are very sensitive to frost. In warm climates, they should be in full sun or light shade. But you may have more success with this plant by keeping it indoors in a sunny window.

Lemongrass

Lemongrass stalks can provide antioxidants such as beta-carotene and a defense against cancer and eye inflammation. Lemongrass has a strong lemon flavor. You can brew it in tea as well as use it as an herb seasoning. To grow this outdoors, you need to live in at least Zone 9. Outside it can grow up to six feet high but will be notably smaller if you grow it indoors.

Bergamot (Bee Balm)

Gaining renewed popularity as a culinary herb, Bee Balm makes a wonderful addition to pizzas, salads, breads and any dishes that are complimented by the herb's unique flavor. Minty and slightly spicy, Bergamot makes a great substitute for Oregano. Bergamot has a long history of use as a medicinal plant by many Native Americans, including the Blackfeet. The Blackfeet Indians used this hardy perennial in poultices to treat minor cuts and wounds. A tea made from the plant was also used to treat mouth and throat infections caused by gingivitis, as the plant contains high levels of a naturally occurring antiseptic, Thymol, which is found in many brand name mouthwashes.

Oregano

Oregano is also part of the mint family and is native to the warm climates of Eurasia and the Mediterranean. Oregano is a perennial plant but in colder climates can be grown as an annual. It is sometimes called wild marjoram and is closely related to sweet marjoram. Oregano is used for flavoring and is a staple herb of Italian American cuisine. In the United States, it gained popularity following World War II as soldiers returned home with a desire for the "pizza herb."

Recipes

Spiced Grilled Chicken with Cilantro Butter

Ingredients

1 tablespoon chili powder

2 teaspoons brown sugar

2 teaspoons Gustus Vitae spicy chocolate cinnamon cane sugar

1/2 teaspoon salt

1/8 teaspoon pepper

3 tablespoons olive oil

1 tablespoon balsamic vinegar

6 bone-in chicken breast halves (8 ounces each)

CILANTRO LIME BUTTER:

1/3 cup butter, melted

1/4 cup minced fresh cilantro

2 tablespoons finely chopped red onion

1 tablespoon lime juice

1 serrano pepper, finely chopped

1/8 teaspoon pepper

In a small bowl, combine the first seven ingredients. Brush over chicken.

Place chicken skin side down on grill rack. Grill, covered, over indirect medium heat for 15 minutes. Turn; grill 20-25 minutes longer or until a meat thermometer reads 165°.

Meanwhile, in a small bowl, combine the butter ingredients. Drizzle over chicken before serving.

Nutrition Facts

1 chicken breast half with 1 tablespoon lime butter: 426 calories, 27g fat (10g saturated fat), 138mg cholesterol, 411mg sodium, 4g carbohydrate (3g sugars, 1g fiber), 40g protein.

Rosemary Salmon and Veggies

Ingredients

1-1/2 pounds salmon fillets, cut into 4 portions

2 tablespoons melted coconut oil or olive oil

2 tablespoons balsamic vinegar

2 teaspoons minced fresh rosemary or 3/4 teaspoon dried rosemary, crushed

1 garlic clove, minced

1/2 teaspoon salt

1 pound fresh asparagus, trimmed

1 medium sweet red pepper, cut into 1-inch pieces

1/4 teaspoon pepper

Lemon wedges

Directions

Preheat oven to 400°. Place salmon in a greased 15x10x1-in. baking pan. Combine oil, vinegar, rosemary, garlic and salt. Pour half over salmon. Place asparagus and red pepper in a large bowl; drizzle with remaining oil mixture and toss to coat. Arrange around salmon in pan; sprinkle with pepper.

Bake until salmon flakes easily with a fork and vegetables are tender, 12-15 minutes. Serve with lemon wedges.

Nutrition Facts

1 serving: 357 calories, 23g fat (9g saturated fat), 85mg cholesterol, 388mg sodium, 7g carbohydrate (4g sugars, 2g fiber), 31g protein. Diabetic Exchanges: 4 lean meat, 1-1/2 fat, 1

Orange Blossom Mint Refresher

Ingredients

20 cups water

1 bunch fresh mint (about 1 cup)

1 cup sugar

1 large navel orange

1 to 2 tablespoons orange blossom water or 1-1/2 to 2-1/2 teaspoons orange extract

Optional: Orange slices and additional fresh mint

Directions

Place water and mint in a 6-qt. slow cooker. Cover and cook on high until heated through, about 6 hours. Strain tea; discard mint.

Whisk in sugar until dissolved. Cut orange crosswise in half; squeeze juice from orange. Stir in juice and orange blossom water. Transfer to a pitcher. Refrigerate until cold, 4-6 hours. Serve over ice with orange slices and additional mint, if desired.

Test Kitchen tips

Orange blossom water, also called orange flower water, can be found at most specialty grocery stores or spice shops.

Using orange extract instead of orange blossom will add a hint of orange flavor, while blossom water adds a unique floral note.

Nutrition Facts

1 cup: 43 calories, 0 fat (0 saturated fat), 0 cholesterol, 0 sodium, 11g carbohydrate (11g sugars, 0 fiber), 0 protein.

Blueberry, Basil and Goat Cheese Pie

Ingredients

Pastry for single-crust pie (9 inches)

2 cups fresh blueberries

2 tablespoons plus 2 teaspoons sugar, divided

1 tablespoon cornstarch

1 tablespoon minced fresh basil

1 large egg

1 teaspoon water

1/4 cup crumbled goat cheese

Fresh basil leaves, torn

Directions

Preheat oven to 375°. On a floured sheet of parchment, roll dough into a 10-in. circle. Transfer to a baking sheet.

Mix blueberries, 2 tablespoons sugar, cornstarch and basil. Spoon blueberry mixture over pastry to within 2 in. of edge. Fold pastry edge over filling, pleating as you go and leaving the center uncovered.

Whisk egg and water; brush over pastry. Sprinkle with remaining sugar. Bake 30 minutes. Sprinkle with goat cheese; bake until crust is golden and filling is bubbly, about 10 minutes.

Transfer to a wire rack to cool. Top with torn basil leaves before serving.

Pastry for single-crust pie (9 inches): Combine 1-1/4 cups all-purpose flour and 1/4 tsp. salt; cut in 1/2 cup cold butter until crumbly. Gradually add 3-5 Tbsp. ice water, tossing with a fork until dough holds together when pressed. Wrap in plastic wrap and refrigerate 1 hour.

Nutrition Facts

1 piece: 308 calories, 18g fat (11g saturated fat), 77mg cholesterol, 241mg sodium, 34g carbohydrate (11g sugars, 2g fiber), 5g protein.

Herbed Feta Dip

Ingredients

1/2 cup packed fresh parsley sprigs

1/2 cup fresh mint leaves

1/2 cup olive oil

2 garlic cloves, peeled

1/2 teaspoon pepper

4 cups (16 ounces) crumbled feta cheese

3 tablespoons lemon juice

Assorted fresh vegetables

Directions

In a food processor, combine the first five ingredients; cover and pulse until finely chopped. Add cheese and lemon juice; process until creamy. Serve with vegetables.

Nutrition Facts

1/4 cup: 176 calories, 15g fat (5g saturated fat), 20mg cholesterol, 361mg sodium, 2g carbohydrate (0 sugars, 1g fiber), 7g protein.

Cauliflower Dill Kugel

Ingredients

5 tablespoons butter, divided

1-1/2 cups thinly sliced shallots

4 large eggs

2 cups whole-milk ricotta cheese

1 cup minced fresh parsley, divided

1/2 cup shredded Gruyere or Swiss cheese

1/4 cup dill weed, divided

3 teaspoons grated lemon zest, divided

1/4 teaspoon salt, divided

1/8 teaspoon pepper

1 package (16 ounces) frozen cauliflower, thawed and patted dry

3/4 cup panko bread crumbs

1/2 teaspoon garlic powder

Directions

Preheat oven to 375°. In a large skillet, heat 3 tablespoons butter over medium-high heat. Add shallots; cook and stir until golden brown, 3-5 minutes. Remove and set aside.

In a large bowl, mix eggs, ricotta cheese, 3/4 cup parsley, shredded cheese, 3 tablespoons dill, 2 teaspoons lemon zest, 1/8 teaspoon salt and pepper. Stir in cauliflower and shallots. Transfer to a greased 8-in. square baking dish.

In the same skillet, heat remaining butter. Add bread crumbs; cook and stir until lightly browned, 2-3 minutes. Stir in garlic powder and the remaining parsley, dill, lemon zest and salt. Sprinkle over cauliflower mixture.

Bake, uncovered, until set, 35-45 minutes. Let stand 10 minutes before cutting. Refrigerate leftovers.

Nutrition Facts

1 piece: 289 calories, 19g fat (11g saturated fat), 147mg cholesterol, 343mg sodium, 16g carbohydrate (7g sugars, 3g fiber), 16g protein.

Cinnamon-Basil Ice Cream

Ingredients

1-1/4 cups whole milk

12 fresh basil leaves

1 cinnamon stick (3 inches)

1/2 cup sugar

4 large egg yolks, lightly beaten

3/4 cup heavy whipping cream

1/4 teaspoon vanilla extract

Ground cinnamon, optional

Directions

In a small saucepan, heat milk to 175°. Remove from the heat; add basil and cinnamon stick. Cover and steep 30 minutes. Strain, discarding basil and cinnamon stick.

Return to the heat; stir in sugar until dissolved. Whisk a small amount of the hot mixture into egg yolks. Return all to the pan, whisking constantly. Cook and stir over low heat until mixture is just thick enough to coat a metal spoon and a thermometer reads at least 160°, stirring constantly. Do not allow to boil. Remove from heat immediately.

Quickly transfer to a large bowl; place bowl in a pan of ice water. Stir gently and occasionally until cool, about 5 minutes. Stir in cream and vanilla. Press plastic wrap onto surface of custard. Refrigerate several hours or overnight.

Fill cylinder of ice cream maker no more than two-thirds full; freeze according to manufacturer's directions. (Refrigerate any remaining mixture until ready to freeze.)

Transfer ice cream to freezer containers, allowing headspace for expansion. Freeze until firm, 2-4 hours.

If desired, sprinkle with ground cinnamon.

Nutrition Facts

1/2 cup: 353 calories, 23g fat (13g saturated fat), 243mg cholesterol, 53mg sodium, 31g carbohydrate (30g sugars, 0 fiber), 6g protein.

Flaky Biscuits with Herb Butter

Ingredients

2 cups all-purpose flour

3 teaspoons baking powder

1 tablespoon sugar

1-1/2 teaspoons minced fresh chives

1-1/2 teaspoons minced fresh tarragon

1 teaspoon salt

1/2 teaspoon garlic powder

1/2 cup shortening

3/4 cup 2% milk

HERB BUTTER:

1/2 cup butter, softened

1-1/2 teaspoons minced fresh chives

1-1/2 teaspoons minced fresh tarragon

1/2 teaspoon garlic powder

Directions

In a small bowl, combine the first 7 ingredients. Cut in shortening until mixture resembles coarse crumbs. Stir in milk just until moistened. Turn onto a lightly floured surface; knead 8-10 times.

Pat or roll out to 1/2-in. thickness; cut with a floured 2-1/2-in. biscuit cutter. Place 2 in. apart on an ungreased baking sheet.

Bake at 425° for 8-12 minutes or until golden brown.

Meanwhile, in a small bowl, beat the butter ingredients until blended; serve with warm biscuits.

Nutrition Facts

1 biscuit with 2 teaspoons butter: 229 calories, 16g fat (7g saturated fat), 21mg cholesterol, 359mg sodium, 18g carbohydrate (2g sugars, 1g fiber), 3g protein.

Chicken and Broccoli with Dill Sauce

Ingredients

4 boneless skinless chicken breast halves (6 ounces each)

1/2 teaspoon garlic salt

1/4 teaspoon pepper

1 tablespoon olive oil

4 cups fresh broccoli florets

1 cup chicken broth

1 tablespoon all-purpose flour

1 tablespoon snipped fresh dill

1 cup 2% milk

Directions

Sprinkle chicken with garlic salt and pepper. In a large skillet, heat oil over medium heat; brown chicken on both sides. Remove from pan.

Add broccoli and broth to same skillet; bring to a boil. Reduce heat; simmer, covered, until broccoli is just tender, 3-5 minutes. Using a slotted spoon, remove broccoli from pan, reserving broth. Keep broccoli warm.

In a small bowl, mix flour, dill and milk until smooth; stir into broth in pan. Bring to a boil, stirring constantly; cook and stir until thickened, 1-2 minutes. Add chicken; cook, covered, over medium heat until a thermometer inserted in chicken reads 165°, 10-12 minutes. Serve with broccoli.

Test Kitchen tips

If you're buying whole broccoli stalks, don't throw out the stems! Peel away the tough outer portion and chop the center to use in soups and stir-fries or add to salads and slaws.

Fresh sugar snap peas would also work well in this recipe; adjust the cooking time as needed.

Nutrition Facts

1 serving: 274 calories, 9g fat (2g saturated fat), 100mg cholesterol, 620mg sodium, 8g carbohydrate (4g sugars, 2g fiber), 39g protein. Diabetic Exchanges: 5 lean meat, 1 vegetable, 1 fat.

Cheddar and Chive Mashed Potatoes

Ingredients

5 pounds Yukon Gold potatoes, peeled and cut into 1-inch pieces (about 10 cups)

1 cup butter, cubed

1 cup sour cream

2 teaspoons salt

3/4 teaspoon pepper

1/2 cup heavy whipping cream

1-1/2 cups shredded cheddar cheese

1-1/2 cups shredded Monterey Jack cheese

1/4 cup grated Parmesan cheese

2 tablespoons minced fresh chives

TOPPINGS:

1 cup shredded cheddar cheese

1 can (6 ounces) french-fried onions

Directions

Place potatoes in a 6-qt. stockpot; add water to cover. Bring to a boil. Reduce heat to medium; cook, uncovered, until tender, 10-15 minutes. Drain; transfer to a large bowl.

Add butter, sour cream, salt and pepper; beat until blended. Beat in whipping cream. Stir in cheeses and chives. Transfer to a 13x9-in. baking dish. Refrigerate, covered, overnight.

To serve, preheat oven to 350°. Remove potatoes from refrigerator while oven heats.

Bake, covered, 45 minutes, stirring after 30 minutes. Sprinkle with toppings; bake, uncovered, until heated through, about 15 minutes.

Test Kitchen Tips

Take care not to overbeat the potatoes; they'll go from whipped to gluey.

Removing the potatoes from the fridge while the oven preheats will warm the potatoes and the dish up a bit. Putting a cold dish directly into a hot oven can cause it to crack.

Nutrition Facts

3/4 cup: 474 calories, 32g fat (18g saturated fat), 70mg cholesterol, 693mg sodium, 37g carbohydrate (3g sugars, 2g fiber), 11g protein.

Golden Beet and Peach Soup with Tarragon

Ingredients

2 pounds fresh golden beets, peeled and cut into 1-inch cubes

1 tablespoon olive oil

2 cups white grape-peach juice

2 tablespoons cider vinegar

1/4 cup plain Greek yogurt

1/4 teaspoon finely chopped fresh tarragon

2 medium fresh peaches, peeled and diced

Fresh tarragon sprigs

Directions

Preheat oven to 400°. Place beets in a 15x10x1-in. baking pan. Drizzle with oil; toss to coat. Roast until tender, 40-45 minutes. Cool slightly.

Transfer beets to a blender or food processor. Add juice and vinegar; process until smooth. Refrigerate at least 1 hour. In a small bowl, combine Greek yogurt and chopped tarragon; refrigerate.

To serve, divide beet mixture among individual bowls; place a spoonful of yogurt mixture in each bowl. Top with diced peaches and tarragon sprigs.

Test Kitchen tips

For a whole different taste sensation, substitute ½ tsp. chopped fresh basil, fresh thyme or fresh chives for the tarragon.

If you prefer, you can blend the herb of your choice with the beets rather than mixing it with the yogurt.

For a creamier soup, add more plain Greek yogurt.

Nutrition Facts

2/3 cup: 159 calories, 4g fat (1g saturated fat), 3mg cholesterol, 129mg sodium, 31g carbohydrate (26g sugars, 4g fiber), 3g protein. Diabetic Exchanges: 2 vegetable, 1 fruit, 1/2 fat.

Rosemary and Ginger Infused Water

Ingredients

2 quarts water

3 fresh rosemary sprigs

1 tablespoon minced fresh gingerroot

Directions

Combine all ingredients in a large glass carafe or pitcher. Cover and refrigerate 12-24 hours. Strain before serving.

Test Kitchen tip

Gently crush fresh herbs, toast dry spices or lightly muddle fresh fruit to get the most flavor in the water.

Herbed Tuna and White Bean Salad

Ingredients

4 cups fresh arugula

1 can (15 ounces) no-salt-added cannellini beans, rinsed and drained

1 cup grape tomatoes, halved

1/2 small red onion, thinly sliced

1/3 cup chopped roasted sweet red peppers

1/3 cup pitted Nicoise or other olives

1/4 cup chopped fresh basil

3 tablespoons extra virgin olive oil

1/2 teaspoon grated lemon zest

2 tablespoons lemon juice

1 garlic clove, minced

1/8 teaspoon salt

2 cans (5 ounces each) albacore white tuna in water, drained

Directions

Place first seven ingredients in a large bowl. Whisk together oil, lemon zest, lemon juice, garlic and salt; drizzle over salad. Add tuna and toss gently to combine.

Test Kitchen tips

Kalamata olives, though stronger in flavor, would be a good substitute for Nicoise olives.

Extra virgin olive oil adds a subtle fruity flavor to the dressing, but plain olive oil could be used instead.

Nutrition Facts

2 cups: 319 calories, 16g fat (2g saturated fat), 30mg cholesterol, 640mg sodium, 20g carbohydrate (3g sugars, 5g fiber), 23g protein. Diabetic Exchanges: 3 fat, 2 lean meat, 1 starch, 1 vegetable.

Cilantro Lime Shrimp

Ingredients

1/3 cup chopped fresh cilantro

1-1/2 teaspoons grated lime zest

1/3 cup lime juice

1 jalapeno pepper, seeded and minced

2 tablespoons olive oil

3 garlic cloves, minced

1/4 teaspoon salt

1/4 teaspoon ground cumin

1/4 teaspoon pepper

1 pound uncooked shrimp (16-20 per pound), peeled and deveined

Lime slices

Directions

Mix first 9 ingredients; toss with shrimp. Let stand 15 minutes.

Thread shrimp and lime slices onto 4 metal or soaked wooden skewers. Grill, covered, over medium heat until shrimp turn pink, 2-4 minutes per side.

Nutrition Facts

1 kabob: 167 calories, 8g fat (1g saturated fat), 138mg cholesterol, 284mg sodium, 4g carbohydrate (1g sugars, 0 fiber), 19g protein. Diabetic Exchanges: 3 lean meat, 1-1/2 fat.

Basil Salt

Ingredients

1/4 cup coarse sea salt

1/4 cup loosely packed basil leaves

Buy Ingredients

Preheat oven to 225°. Place salt and basil in a small food processor; pulse until very finely chopped. Spread into a parchment-lined 15x10x1-in. baking pan.

Bake until mixture appears dry, about 30 minutes. Remove from oven; cool completely in pan. Store in an airtight container at room temperature.

Nutrition Facts

1/4 teaspoon: 0 calories, 0 fat (0 saturated fat), 0 cholesterol, 480mg sodium, 0 carbohydrate (0 sugars, 0 fiber), 0 protein.

Dilly Cheese Ball

Ingredients

1 package (8 ounces) cream cheese, softened

1 cup dill pickle relish, drained

1/4 cup finely chopped onion

1-1/2 cups shredded cheddar cheese

1 tablespoon Worcestershire sauce

2 tablespoons mayonnaise

2 tablespoons minced fresh parsley

Assorted crackers

Directions

Beat first six ingredients until smooth. Shape into a ball; wrap in plastic. Refrigerate several hours. Sprinkle with parsley; serve with crackers.

Nutrition Facts

2 tablespoons: 100 calories, 8g fat (4g saturated fat), 22mg cholesterol, 244mg sodium, 5g carbohydrate (1g sugars, 0 fiber), 3g protein.

Green Beans and Radish Salad with Tarragon Pesto

Ingredients

1-1/2 pounds fresh green beans, trimmed

2 cups thinly sliced radishes

1/2 cup pecan or walnut pieces, toasted

1/4 cup tarragon leaves

3 tablespoons grated Parmesan cheese

1/2 garlic clove

1/4 teaspoon coarse sea salt or kosher salt

1/8 teaspoon crushed red pepper flakes

1-1/2 teaspoons white wine vinegar

1/4 cup olive oil

Directions

In a 6-qt. stockpot, bring 8 cups water to a boil. Add beans in batches; cook, uncovered, 2-3 minutes or just until crisp-tender. Remove beans and immediately drop into ice water. Drain and pat dry. Toss together beans and radishes.

Place pecans, tarragon, cheese, garlic, salt and pepper flakes in a small food processor; pulse until chopped. Add vinegar; process until blended. Continue processing while gradually adding oil in a steady stream. Toss with bean mixture.

Nutrition Facts

1 cup: 115 calories, 10g fat (1g saturated fat), 1mg cholesterol, 89mg sodium, 7g carbohydrate (2g sugars, 3g fiber), 2g protein. Diabetic Exchanges: 2 fat, 1 vegetable.

Peach-Basil Lemonade Slush

Ingredients

2 cups sugar

3 cups chopped peeled fresh peaches (about 3 medium) or 1 pound frozen unsweetened sliced peaches

1 package (3/4 ounce) fresh basil leaves or 20 large leaves

4 cups water

1-1/2 cups fresh lemon juice

5 to 8 cups ice cubes

Peach slices and fresh basil leaves

Directions

In a large saucepan, combine sugar, peaches, basil and water; bring to a boil. Reduce heat; simmer 5 minutes. Remove from heat; let stand 30 minutes. Discard basil; stir in lemon juice. Refrigerate until cooled completely.

Process half of peach mixture and 2-1/2 cups ice in a blender until blended, adding more ice if desired. Repeat with remaining peach mixture and ice. Pour into chilled glasses; serve with peach slices and basil.

Nutrition Facts

1 cup: 152 calories, 0 fat (0 saturated fat), 0 cholesterol, 1mg sodium, 39g carbohydrate (37g sugars, 1g fiber), 1g protein.

Apricot-Rosemary Scones

Ingredients

4 cups all-purpose flour

2 tablespoons sugar

2 tablespoons baking powder

3/4 teaspoon salt

1-1/2 cups cold butter, cubed

1 cup chopped dried apricots

1 tablespoon minced fresh rosemary

4 large eggs, room temperature, lightly beaten

1 cup cold heavy whipping cream

TOPPING:

1 large egg, lightly beaten

2 tablespoons 2% milk

2 teaspoons sugar

Directions

Preheat oven to 400°. Whisk together flour, sugar, baking powder and salt. Cut in cold butter until the size of peas. Stir in apricots and rosemary.

In a separate bowl, whisk eggs and whipping cream until blended. Stir into flour-butter mixture just until moistened.

Turn onto a well-floured surface. Roll dough into a 10-in. square. Cut into 4 squares; cut each square into 4 triangles. Place on baking sheets lined with parchment.

For topping, combine egg and milk. Brush tops of scones with egg mixture; sprinkle with sugar. Bake until golden brown, 12-15 minutes.

Freeze option: Freeze cooled scones in resealable freezer containers. To use, reheat in a preheated 350° oven 20-25 minutes, adding time as necessary to heat through.

Nutrition Facts

1 scone: 372 calories, 25g fat (15g saturated fat), 121mg cholesterol, 461mg sodium, 32g carbohydrate (7g sugars, 1g fiber), 6g protein.

Honey-Thyme Butter

Ingredients

1/2 cup butter, softened

1/3 cup honey

2 teaspoons fresh thyme leaves

Buy Ingredients

Powered by Chicory

Directions

In a small bowl, beat the butter until light and fluffy. Add the honey and thyme; beat just until blended. Store in refrigerator.

Nutrition Facts

1 tablespoon: 58 calories, 5g fat (3g saturated fat), 12mg cholesterol, 37mg sodium, 5g carbohydrate (5g sugars, 0 fiber), 0 protein.

Bottom line

Fresh and dried herbs can add new flavours and aromas to your cooking without added fat, sodium or calories. Experiment with the different herbs to see what you like best.

Printed in Great Britain
by Amazon